Tertium Quid

Trivius Caldwell

BookLeaf
Publishing

India | USA | UK

Presentation by *BookLeaf Publishing*

Web: www.bookleafpub.com

E-mail: info@bookleafpub.com

ISBN: 9789360942694

First edition 2024

Torrent

Montgomery told me that my eyes were sad, but that was a few days ago when I remembered how William's eyes smiled. I hope I can cry today. The rain is heavy so maybe I can hide under its cloak. I only have a couple of minutes, so on with it. Cry havoc or cry peace? Doesn't matter because memory folds time like fabric. Memory cuts through water like a current. I've learned that tears cannot hold smiles. William once noticed my eyes smiling. He hugged me and whispered, "All the Way" sir! I put those memories in the "down there" of my mind, and the rain helps me flood them out. But William is gone, so I must be quick. My boys depend on it. They tell me men do not cry, but Soldiers do. And I believed them. I kept camouflage face paint close, to smear my mask, so I can cry in the rain. No more though…let it flow.

He carried polished pebbles.
Water flows through
but not inside.

…Night Raid…

We saw our sighs that day. After a moment of silence, we put chaos behind us and walked through breath clouds toward the next objective. We sent the fallen home and weaved down the frozen dirt road to the adobe, looking for the bombmaker. It could have been hot sand, dirty snow, or hard rocks in the Hindu Kush mountains, but on that chilly dark night, through green ocular frames, we saw farmland, mud huts, and moon glare. The door was not locked. And we were quiet, yet the bombmaker ran anyway. We could catch him with well-aimed fire or frigid feet. The latter is cleaner but hard, so we gave chase. Running turns sighs into gasps, and vengeance is not ours because he lived and... It is better this way, because children do not wake and cry when Soldiers run in frozen mud. When we shoot, they sob. We manage violence and our souls suffers. Night vision helps and makes the world glow, but our sighs fog the world. We saw our sighs the next night, and after a moment of silence, we walked again.

They are home
in folded flags. 'Neath green grass
and betwixt stars.

Lillies

I want to miss you, but I don't. Your absence is so present that I consider it a gift. All I remember is the smell of vanilla wood from the mahogany furniture in the courtroom. Three decades ago, you denied your blood from that mahogany bench: "Those are not my children." I remember that declaration. Today, I heard the question in your voice when you described how my children had grown—you did not ask about your grandchildren. Indeed, they have, and so have I. My television fathers couldn't talk to me after we found that thing in the woods. They couldn't keep me from cutting school to watch and read things. I wish someone could explain what we were seeing that day. I wish someone had explained how seeds grow without water. Your absence propelled mom into a maternal everything. She nurtured self-reliance like a gardener tending a Crown Vetch. She tried to be everywhere at once, but my brothers and I spread like the Vetch, and her garden quickly become overgrown. We were everywhere and nowhere, and you watched us in this void. I must thank you for your absence, since the void established a blank slate…a worldly canvas to make space. Enter every thing, and we lived everything. I think I miss the idea of what your presence could bring, but then again, your presence would deny water from other spouts. I spoke of forgiveness when I realized the question you did not ask. The embarrassment in your voice, in my head, sounded like that alarm when we got caught stealing underwear after we watched the thing. This reminds me that even young children are aware of their nakedness. They suffer drought too.

Flightless birds and
lavender Crown petals
flourish in spite of.

Quiet As Kept

Amiri Baraka wrote
"Black Art."
"We want a black poem. And a
Black World.
Let the world be a Black Poem
And Let All Black People Speak This Poem
Silently
Or LOUD."

I remember chasing rainbows. This is not
hyperbole.
I drove to the end of a rainbow and saw it miles
away.
Black boy joy is like that.

Sth.

Black Boy Joy Ain't.

I Mean. It ain't real. It ain't safe. It ain't
something I can close my eyes and paint. The
boy's Blackness must be the nothing that is
everything. The light in the tunnel, or maybe the
end of it.

I'm told there is light in Black space. In a Black world.

Black boys cry. Run. Jump. Sing. Black boys smile. Walk. Crawl. Black boys fight. Weep. Black boys die.
There were no rainbows when Tamir, Trayvon, Triv…It almost happened thrice.

That's when joy ended. When the blackness of the barrel gave way to the bullet. The tunnels light pushed by gunpower. It missed me twice. Black boy joy had to go. Smiles and cries can't live in my hood. Black boy joy had work hours. On shift, Black boy joy believed in rainbows. Pot of gold they said. We chased treasure and found nothing.

Black boy joy ain't because black boys must protect their souls. Black boys fear. Black boys are afraid. Black boys hide. In my hood, Black boys watched police beat Black brothers. Black sisters watch and hide secrets too. Their joy fight fears. Black girl magic?

Between me and the world. Black boys think about white boys. The girls watch and all the boys grin. Fear fights joy if the Black boy notices white skin. Who took it? What took the

joy? Is it there? When Black boys thought they
were brown? When white children asked about
black hair? When white girls touched my
daughter's hair? Where is that joy? When smiles
and cries stood in for words? Or before the
switch reminded Black boys to mind their body.

I'm told to find the little Black boy inside me.
Listen to him and give him grace. The little
Black boy lives rent free and happy because the
joy in him is in me.

Joy defies shadows in the color of nothing.
Joy ain't got no color. Can't live translucent.
Can you see? What is it?

This joy…Black boy joy, ain't. It is. Quiet and
Kept.

Black Is and Black Ain't

Black is Beautiful
Black girls
Black braid
Black hair
Black like
Black rivers.

Black People
Black shine
Black like
Black gold
Black crowns.

Black Butterfly
Black flies
Black toward
Black skies.

Black Lives
Black matter.
Black thought
Black splatter.

Black is Beautiful
Black boys

Black play
Black music.

Black is and
Black ain't.
Black gives
Black takes.

Black is Beautiful…

"Hey Daddy!"
Yes Black Baby?

"We're Brown!"

Pirouette

The wind is soft this morning and burnt rust
rests in its fog. Children smile and skip under
geese while squirrels make way for morning's
amble. The forest bends into a wall behind the
fog, beyond cool dew, a winding trail sits quiet.
Lean in and ride the wind. It lifts and bends and
breaks. The forest wall is yellow and canary this
time of year. Hello peace and tumult. Hello
breeze and serenity. Hello dew and dirt. Behind
the fog is life's noise. And children dare not
venture beyond. The space belongs to someone.
Peace. Breeze. Dew. It belongs to someone. In
that quiet expanse, Mother nature orchestrates a
delicate dance. Children cannot understand the
gold wall whispers. They are stories only the
wise understand.

Soft morning zephyr
helps the vulture smell
its prey.

Speculum Nudus

Who told you that you were naked?

The world beholds you, and so do I. Do not
despair, for life emerged in the raw, and in the
raw, life shall conclude. Veil yourself, and gazes
may subside. But you—unyielding, you avert no
glance. Look upon and love.

Adorn yourself for the world, a mirror reflecting
its essence! Whose visage do I discern? Are we
mere reflections in life's looking glass, molded
into preconceived imaginings?

Suppress desire, and remorse takes root.
Remorse burgeons into trauma, a venom that
taints that garden.

No sanctuary thrives in that garden!
Blossoms unfurl clandestinely, akin to concealed
grandchildren.

The Almighty inquired of man, delving into the
intricacies of his corporeal form.

"Who declared you naked?"

"Did you peer into a mirror and surmise kindred
souls?"
"Do puddles linger still in the garden?"

Those mirrors cast reflections of the
sublime—azure skies and undraped truth.

Men attire themselves in the shroud of fear.
In the mirrors of other eyes, they seek their own
reflection.

When He proclaimed your nakedness, you
embraced the belief.
Away you rushed to seize concealment. You
became a flower of that garden.

Reveal not your exquisite skin; revel instead in
nakedness, in the genesis of being.
Lean into the love that ensues, and luxuriate in
the intimacy that sustains eternal query:

Who told you that you were naked?
Discern that voice.

Shaka

In the sun-kissed savannah, shadows dance across tall grass, weaving tales of Shaka's enduring legacy. Heat hangs heavy while a humid shroud embraced the warrior king's spectral presence.

The sun paints shadows on the tall grass on the hot and humid prairie. Shaka orchestrated the Impi's dance with the spear while trampling that grass. As ancestral drums echoed a rhythm of resistance under acacia trees, the ghostly whispers of regiments past linger. Iklwa spears now project bullets, a poignant shift denying warrior's the intimacy of close combat. Shaka redefined warfare in Africa. The double envelopment became unstoppable and gave way to conquest. The Zulu military machine is a testament to Shaka's brillance. It lives on in the rhythm of the land. In unison, ancestral drums cadencing tales of valor, resistance, and love. The soul of African soil, a soldier's heartbeat pulses in red, akin to the hue of the African sun—Africa's son—Amazulu.

Metal spears clang and Warriors stomp.
Legacy lives
in shadows of the sun.

Ka'ena Point

I stood atop a cascading slope, amidst silent roars of thought, random musings cascade like whispers in the wind. Sloshing ocean water pushed my mind beyond. Contemplating the letter beyond Z, the realm of the unknown is approachable. Boundaries dissolve into infinity and the ocean's blue is magnificent.

An analog clock, no numbers, just a metaphor for the timeless expanse of existence. It spirals endlessly into the void. Into the nowhere. Into Erehwon.

Do fish ponder their place in water? Their world unfathomable without fluid embrace. And what of the revelation of air, to them, a foreign realm beckoning beyond the shimmering surface? In the midst of existential queries, a longing stirs—yearning for connection, pleading for understanding. Who is the elusive 'you' who remains a mystery yet to be unveiled. Who is the me myself?

As above and so below. The stars twinkle in the vast expanse. The ache of absence lingers like a shadow in the moonlight. Amidst a paradox of plenty and lack, questions linger like ghosts in the corridors of my mind, haunting the present with echoes of the past.

"I see you. I've seen you."

Beside oneself, lost in recollection, reflections of past time beckon from the depths. In the gaze upon the world, there lies a longing to grasp the ineffable, to transcend the limitations of language and perception, and to embrace the enigma of existence with eyes wide open.

Beyond the veil of illusion, beneath the cascading torrents of life's flow, lies the elusive truth—ever-shifting, ever-elusive, beckoning to be uncovered. Unraveled certainty, questioning reality, the essence of revelation sits right here.

It dances with the light and shadow, in the interplay of thought and emotion. The journey of self-discovery is a pilgrimage of the soul, guided by muses who whisper, "Know thyself."

Random musings drift
Whispers in the silent void
Seeking truth beyond.

Night Shift

In the heart of war's abyss, we searched for his vanished body. AWOL! He was swallowed by the shadow. His body torn by the explosive. Silence followed the chaos, a chilling echo of the horror we faced. Talks of horror morphed into dissonance. We find other things to talk about.

The little green men patrolled and searched in the infrared glow. Afghanistan's landscape unfolded through a symphony of dust storms and frigid dirt, punctuated by distant explosions. Amidst the turmoil, memories of home clashed with the harsh reality of war's grip. The Graveyard of Empires had again bore witness to the fallen, a solemn reminder of the price paid in blood—it flows through the vein of our world with vigor, warm and thick. It tattoos our armor so we won't forget. Blood holds no reflection. It pools with dirt and clots the earth. Soldiers trot over thrombus, toward the enemy, pooling more paths home.

Breath clouds till bloody soil.
Butterflies land on
shards of glass.

Toni

Tonight, the wind sounds familiar. It's timbre is
Toni Morrison. The wind wisps and whispers. It
sings silent and cools carefully. Take your time
and understand how the breeze touches you.
Feel Wind's tingle and inhale. And maybe you
might hear your soul singing songs of solace.
We need that sometimes. Listen to your soul and
seek solitude. Seek comfort in loneliness. "My
lonely is mine. Now your lonely is somebody
else's. Made by somebody else and handed to
you. Ain't that something? A secondhand
lonely." Ain't that something, wind that waits on
you.

Night whispers Wind's hymn.
Sings melodies of care.
And she was loved.

Runaway Fred

"Ten Dollars Reward. For the apprehension of a Mulatto Slave named FRED He is about 16 or 18 years old, very well grown, and in height from five feet 7 to 10 inches high, rather slim for his height, has a mulatto complexion and a bashful countenance; his hair naturally curls, but lately has been cut close to his head. He is very artful and ingenious, and has passed himself as free-born in this place, and will endeavour to procure a free pass. He took off with him a Japan hat, a black broad cloth coat, mixed surtcoat and other good clothes. It supposed his objective will be to get to a sea port, (probably Edenton or Plymouth) in order to get off in some vessel; or he will shape his course of Sampson County and Wilmington, where he was raised. I will give the above reward to any person who will confine him in any jail, and give me information of the same, or Thomas Burgess or John R. Leigh, Esq. so that I get him again. Captains of vessels are requested to keep a look out and secure said boy. William H. Williams Halifax (N.C.) June 27, 1820."

"I'm looking for a slave in a Japanese hat?"
"Ten Dollar Reward. For the apprehension of a
Mulatto Slave named Fred." You ain't gon' find
'em. Fred be everywhere and nowhere, slick as
they come. He got that genius mind, crafty as a
fox. Rockin' that black broad coat, fresh cut, and
a Japanese hat like it's nothin'. Bad nigga, ain't
it? A teenage runaway, thinkin' 'bout fashion
while dodgin' massa's grip. Got that mulatto
skin, standin' all but 5 foot 8, all confidence.
Good luck catchin' Fred! Fred done vanished!
He done played y'all like fools, makin' y'all think
he a free man. Excuse me, 'free-born.' How
many folks you know down in North Carolina
sportin' a Japanese hat? Ha! Slaves don't wear no
hat from Japan, I'll tell ya that much. But this
here Fred, he different. Found himself some
shade and blendin' in like dem insects. The one
dat change skin. Ha! He warm and long gone!

Ten dollars ain't even close enuf to send Fred
back to Halifax. Keep an eye out for a colored
fella in a Japanese hat! William H. Williams
better cough up that ten dollars for spreadin'
such nonsense!

Fred stowed away.
Took off his shoes.
Slept on that Japanese hat.

Glare

Be a beacon for lost souls.

You were put here to help.
Remember this, especially when you get weary.
For the only strength you need is the belief in
the possibility of change.

Of growth.

Cool

In life's labyrinth, I navigated away from the distasteful, where hands that shaped me could also shatter my being. With caution, I avoided the insidious whispers of evil thoughts seeking to usurp my essence, they aimed to prop me up only to offer me as prey to others. Ambition, a double-edged sword, sowed seeds of suspicion among those around me, they smiled in daylight and conspired in the shadows.

In the twilight realm of deception, I encountered a figure who honed his lies through the practice of mimicry, his strange strategy an unsettling mirror of my own being.

In the ceaseless ebb and flow of existence, I grappled with the weight of my own effort, each word a world. Fragile vessels struggling against the currents of failure. My ego, a treacherous guide, led me into the lair of Medusa herself, where her venomous words burned my soul and coerced my compliance.

Beneath such weight of societal expectation, I excavate emotions deep, confronting the dual nature of pain as both a source of vulnerability and strength. Amidst the tumult, I encountered manifestations of malevolence, insidious forces seeking to manipulate and consume.

In the silence of introspection, I heeded the wisdom of my child's voice, a beacon of clarity in darkness. She warned of those who dwell in the realm of falsehoods and reminded me of the resilience born from the depths of adversity.

The immaculate idea of your genesis is not your born date.

Flight

I was a bird in Madagascar.

Warning

I see you lurking. Watch This.

Unpayable Debt

White Skin,
Black Mask.

Black Pride,
And Brown Skin.

Hip Hop

Smothered

&Covered

&Chunked

&Chopped

&Screwed.

www.ingramcontent.com/pod-product-compliance
Lightning Source LLC
La Vergne TN
LVHW010858200726
843508LV00012B/2931